# VAN GOGH COLORING BOOK VOL. 1

1) Self-Portrait

2) Shoes

3) Irises

4) Bedroom in Arles

5) Starry Night

6) Portrait of Joseph Roulin

7) Sunflowers

8) Girl in white

9) The night café

10) Self-portrait with grey felt hat

11) Wheat field with cypresses

12) Man smoking

1. Self-Portrait -1887

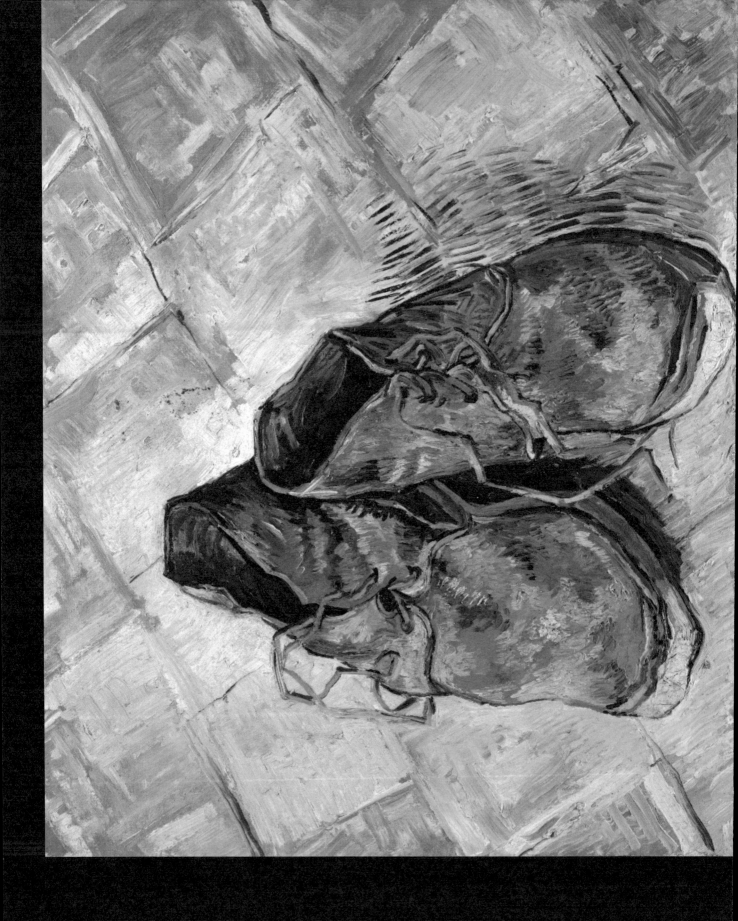

## 2. Shoes  -1888

**3. Irises -1890**

4. Bedroom in Arles -1889

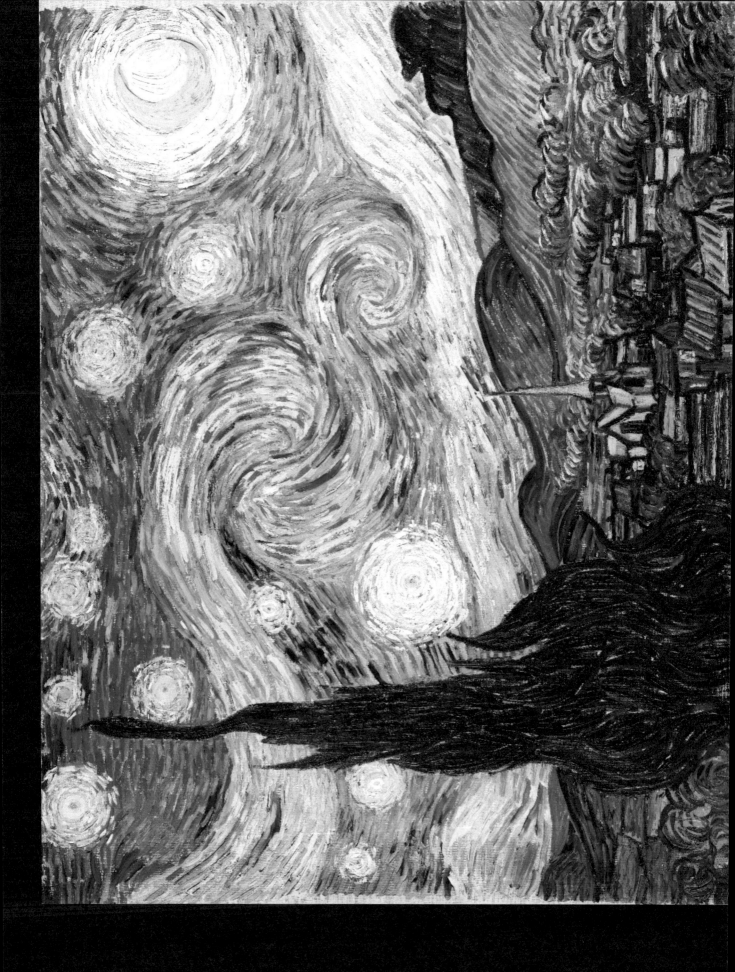

## 5. Starry Night -1889

**6. Portrait of
Joseph Roulin -1889**

# 7. Sunflowers -1888

**8. Girl in white -1890**

**9. The night café -1888**

**10. Self-portrait with grey felt hat -1886-87**

**11.Wheat field
with cypresses - 1889**

**12. Man smoking -1888**

25862676R00019